Beach Detectives

Elen Caldecott

Illustrated by
Alex Paterson

OXFORD
UNIVERSITY PRESS

OXFORD
UNIVERSITY PRESS

Great Clarendon Street, Oxford, OX2 6DP,
United Kingdom

Oxford University Press is a department of the University of Oxford.
It furthers the University's objective of excellence in research, scholarship,
and education by publishing worldwide. Oxford is a registered trade mark of
Oxford University Press in the UK and in certain other countries

Text © Elen Caldecott 2017

Illustrations © Alex Paterson 2017

The moral rights of the author have been asserted

First published 2017

British Library Cataloguing in Publication Data
Data available

978-0-19-837730-6

7 9 10 8 6

Paper used in the production of this book is a natural, recyclable product
made from wood grown in sustainable forests. The manufacturing process
conforms to the environmental regulations of the country of origin.

Printed in China by Golden Cup

Acknowledgements
Inside cover notes written by Karra McFarlane
Author photograph by Blue Material Girl

Contents

Chapter 1
Mystery on the Seashore

"I'm winning!" Glyn barked in delight as he raced ahead of his boy.

"Not for long," Bryn replied. Sand flew up in the air as they hurtled towards Mum, Dad and Bryn's little sister Alis.

"Careful," Mum said, "you'll get sand in the sandwiches!"

"Or bits on the birthday cake!" Dad added. "What have you two detectives been up to? Have you solved any crimes?"

Bryn knew that Dad was only joking, but he and Glyn *had* been hunting for clues on the beach. "We found an old bottle, but it didn't have a message inside. Glyn found a shoe, but we didn't find its owner."

Glyn barked in agreement. Bryn gave him a little wink.

They both collapsed on to the picnic rug.

Alis squealed as Mum emptied the picnic basket. Mum pulled out biscuits and buns, carrots and sandwiches and, best of all, a birthday cake for Alis!

"Four today!" Dad said. He lifted out plastic plates and cups.

Alis dived towards the cake. Her hands stretched to grab it.

Dad scooped Alis up just before her fingers plunged into the sponge. "How about one last paddle before we eat?" he said.

"Yes!" Bryn whooped. Glyn barked. Alis laughed.

Mum nodded. "Come on then."

They splished and sploshed in the gentle waves. Glyn bounded through the foam.

"Don't get too sandy," Bryn warned. "Dad will make you have a bath."

"No!" Glyn cried. "I hate baths!"

Bryn knew the rest of his family couldn't speak Dog. He was the only one who could understand Glyn. And he didn't just speak Dog – he could speak Cat and Pigeon and Hamster and all kinds of other animal languages, too. Seagulls whirled above their heads, and Bryn could hear them yelling at each other to get out of the way.

Then he charged through the surf to splash Dad. "Here I come!" he yelled.

When they were all tired out, Dad said it was time to eat.

"I can't wait to see Alis blow out the candles," Mum said.

They all walked back to the picnic.

"Oh no!" Mum said. "What's happened?"

The picnic was a mess. Plates had tipped over. Juice was spreading in puddles. Sandwiches had fallen open.

Worst of all, Alis's lovely birthday cake was gone!

Alis burst into tears.

"Who could have done this?" Dad gasped.

Bryn caught Glyn's eye.

Glyn nodded. He understood.

This was a mystery, and they were going to solve it.

Chapter 2
A Footprint in the Sand

Alis sobbed. Her eyes were screwed shut and tears splashed down her cheeks.

"There, there," Mum said.

"Hush, hush," Dad soothed.

Bryn knew he and Glyn had to help. Could they find the cake thief and save Alis's birthday party? They had to try.

"We need to examine the area for clues," Bryn said.

"It's a nice thought," Dad said, "but I think it would be better if we packed up and went home. Alis is too upset to celebrate now."

"No!" Bryn pleaded. "Glyn and I can help. I know we can. Please give us a chance."

Dad and Mum looked at each other.

Then Dad said, "It will take a little while for us to pack everything away. You and Glyn can investigate until we're done. But then we're going home. OK?"

Bryn stood, legs wide, hands on his hips. "Bryn and Glyn, Beach Detectives, are on the case. Glyn, hunt for clues."

Glyn dropped his nose to the ground and began to sniff the sand. Bryn eyed the beach. He looked up and down the length of the sand. There were a few other people, lounging on towels, or building sandcastles, or swimming in the sea. None of them was close by. Up near the dunes was a beach cafe. A donkey was giving rides near the surf. Where was the cake thief?

Dad dropped the plates and cups back into the basket. Mum smoothed Alis's hair, trying to stop her tears.

Glyn sniffed at shells and a stray white feather, at a curl of seaweed and a stick. His tail wagged at each new scent. Then he gave an urgent bark. "Bryn! Look!"

Bryn hurried over. Glyn panted eagerly. He had found something.

"What is it?" Bryn asked.

Glyn stepped aside so Bryn could see. In the damp sand was the perfect impression of a U-shaped footprint.

Bryn knew exactly what he was looking at. He felt a bubble of excitement form in his chest. "The beach donkey!" he said.

Chapter 3
The Silence of the Donkey

Dad and Mum wiped sand off the spades
and packed them away. Bryn and Glyn
didn't have long. They ran as quickly
as they could across the beach, hunting
their first suspect.

The beach donkey!

The donkey stood at the water's
edge. He had his head down and his tail
flicked at imaginary flies. His brown
saddle was decorated with ribbons and
tassels, but they looked old and faded.

As they got closer, the donkey sighed. "Oh no, this one looks heavy."

"It's all right," Bryn said, "I don't want a ride."

The donkey lifted his head slowly and stared at Bryn from under sleepy lashes. "Then what *do* you want? Leave me be, I'm very busy."

"You don't look busy," Glyn said.

"I'm busy thinking," the donkey explained. "You're interrupting."

"Can we ask you a few questions?" Bryn said. The waves hissed as they rolled over the sand. Small birds, oystercatchers and sandpipers, yelled above their heads. But the donkey was silent.

"What do you know about a birthday cake that has disappeared from our picnic?" Bryn asked.

The donkey blinked a few times and then answered slowly. "Nothing."

"I found your hoofprint near our picnic blanket!" Glyn insisted.

"Where?" the donkey asked.

"There." Bryn pointed to where Mum and Dad were shaking sand out of the basket.

"Oh," the donkey drawled. "I was there this morning, when the tide was in. That's why my hoofprint is near your blanket, but I haven't been up there for hours."

Bryn felt his excitement drain away, like air from a drooping balloon. Their clue wasn't a clue after all. "Did you see anyone else go near our blanket?"

The donkey dropped his head and stared down, as though the sand was suddenly really interesting.

"What?" Bryn asked. "What do you know?"

"I can't say," the donkey said. "The seagulls will be mean to me."

"Seagulls!" Glyn exclaimed.

The donkey groaned. "Oh, I shouldn't have said anything."

"Were they near the picnic?" Bryn asked.

"I can't say."

"You don't need to be scared of seagulls!" Glyn scoffed.

"You haven't met these seagulls," the donkey said.

"There was a white feather by the picnic, remember?" Glyn said to Bryn.

Bryn nodded. "It was a clue. We need to speak to those seagulls!"

Chapter 4
The Gull on the Bin

There were seagulls circling in the blue
sky above Bryn and Glyn, but there
were many more seagulls outside the
beach cafe.

Bryn and Glyn crossed the sand
quickly, towards the little building by
the dunes. Bryn could see that Mum and
Dad were almost done – he was nearly
out of time.

The cafe was decorated with pictures of ice creams and lollies. A blackboard covered with prices leaned against the wall. Outside was a squat concrete bin. It was there that the seagulls stood, like guards on a castle tower.

Bryn and Glyn slowed to a walk and then stopped.

The biggest seagull had small yellow
eyes and a sharp pointy beak. She turned
her head. The other gulls followed suit.
They were all staring at Bryn and Glyn
now, their eyes narrow.

One squawked, "Strangers!"

Another added, "Trespassers!"

A third cried, "Invaders!"

The whole flock took up the screech.
"Invaders! Invaders!"

Bryn stepped backwards. Glyn's tail curled between his legs.

"Get away from our bins!" the big seagull yelled. She hopped down from the edge of the bin on to the sandy concrete and jabbed her beak into the air angrily.

Bryn rested his hand on Glyn's warm back and took a deep breath. "Did you steal my sister's birthday cake?"

The seagulls cackled. Their laughter
made Bryn tremble. His fingers gripped
Glyn's fur tighter.

The big seagull laughed the loudest.
Then she said, "Everything on this
beach is ours. We're in charge around
here. We take whatever we like and no
one can stop us."

Bryn swallowed hard. It felt as if
there was something caught in his
throat. "Does that mean you did
take it?"

The big seagull howled with laughter. Then she marched closer to Bryn. "Get away!" she snapped. "Get away!"

The other gulls yelled too, in an angry chorus. "Get away! Get away!" Their beaks clacked cruelly. The claws on the tips of their feet clattered as they stamped and bounced.

Bryn and Glyn turned and ran.

Chapter 5
What the Crab Saw

Bryn and Glyn didn't run back to Mum
and Dad. They raced behind a rock and
crouched down, out of sight of the gulls.

"Are you all right?" Bryn asked Glyn.
He nodded quickly. "You?"

"I'm OK, but those seagulls are scary.
The beach donkey was right."

"You don't know the half of it," a small voice suddenly said.

Bryn looked around, but he couldn't see who was speaking. The rock was bare, but there were some sandy pools that had been left behind by the tide.

"Down here!" the voice said again.

Bryn looked down. A small, brown
crab looked up at him, its eyes on stalks.
The crab gave a little wave with its claw.

"Oh, hello. What do you mean?" Bryn
asked. "Why don't I know the half of it?"

"I saw them!" the crab said. "They did steal the cake. They gulped it right down. They were going to steal the rest of your picnic too, if it hadn't been for Carys. She charged right in and scared them off. She was braver than all the rest of us beach animals put together!"

The seagulls had planned to take *everything*? Bryn couldn't believe it. How horrid!

"Who's Carys?" Glyn asked.

"A stray dog," the crab replied. "She lives in a den under the cafe."

"Why don't the beach animals stop the seagulls?" Bryn said.

"I'm a crab! What can I do?"

"I mean all the beach animals," Bryn said. "You and the donkey, the rabbits and voles in the dunes. The sandpipers and oystercatchers. Everyone! You don't know what you can do if you work together."

The crab shook his head and pulled his eyes in.

It was no use.

Glyn nudged Bryn's leg. "The cake's gone. But we should find Carys, to say thank you for trying. It's the least we can do."

Glyn was right. Bryn gave the crab a sad look. It scuttled away.

Bryn and Glyn headed off to search for Carys's den. They had to keep out of sight of the gulls. They kept to the shadow of the dunes and the cafe building.

Eventually, Bryn found what he
was looking for. Some of the wooden
boards that ran along the bottom of
the concrete building were broken.
There were dog prints in the sand
leading inside.

"Carys?" Bryn whispered.

"Carys?" Glyn barked softly.

They heard a scamper. Then a dog
with black patches on her white coat
wriggled out. She gave a friendly woof.
"Hello!"

"We've come to say thank you," Bryn
said. "The crab told us how brave you
were, standing up to those seagulls."

Carys growled. "Those gulls are nothing but trouble. They think they own the beach, but they don't. It's meant to be for everyone."

"Yes," Glyn said, "those seagulls are horrible."

There was a squawk behind them. Bryn and Glyn turned slowly.

The big seagull was standing right behind them, and she had heard every word.

Chapter 6
Along Came a Seagull

The big seagull was staring at Bryn and Glyn menacingly. Behind her, another seagull fluttered down from the rooftop, then another. They were like soldiers ready to do battle.

Bryn felt his hands turn slippery with sweat. The seagulls' beaks looked sharp.

"You can't talk about us like that," the big seagull said. "This is our beach."

Glyn whimpered softly. Carys growled. Bryn stood as bravely as he could manage.

And then they heard the click of claws. They heard the thump of paws. They heard the clop of hooves.

Over the dune came six crabs, five rabbits, four voles, three oystercatchers, two sandpipers and, in front of them all, one old beach donkey, with his nostrils flared.

"Get out of here, seagulls!" the donkey brayed.

The big seagull gave a squawk of alarm.

"Yes! Get out of here," the animals bellowed.

Bryn couldn't believe the noise!

The big seagull squawked again. Then she lifted her wings and shot up into the air. The other gulls rose too, like rockets, going as fast as they could.

In moments, the seagulls were just dots, disappearing into the blue sky.

"Wow!" Bryn said. "You were all amazing. Thank you!"

The crab shimmied forward. "It's us who should be thanking you. You were the one who gave me the idea. On our own, none of us could chase away the gulls. But together? Together we stood a chance."

"Yes!" Bryn said. "The bullies have gone. The beach is yours."

The rabbits hopped for joy.

The sandpipers trilled.

The crab and the donkey began telling each other the story of the day they saved the beach.

45

Bryn and Glyn strolled away from the cafe, into the sunlight.

There was someone else by their side. Carys.

"Are you sure I should come?" Carys asked.

"Yes!" Bryn said. "Alis will want to say thank you too. You saved her sandwiches."

Mum and Dad were ready to go. Everything was packed away. Alis was still sniffing, her cheeks streaked with tears.

Then she saw Bryn, Glyn and Carys walking towards her.

"Doggy!" she said. "Alis's doggy?"

"Carys," Carys barked.

Alis's eyes grew round in astonishment. "The doggy said her name is Carys!" she said.

"Did she?" Mum laughed. "It looks like you two will be good friends."

Bryn knew that today was going to be Alis's best birthday ever.

About the author

I spend a lot of time with my dog. She keeps me company while I write. I often wonder what it is she's thinking. Is it just about walks and sleeping and food? Or has she got all kinds of adventures going on in her imagination too?

If she could talk, then I'd find out! Perhaps we could even set up our own detective agency, solving all the animal crimes in the park where we walk every day. Watch out, sneaky squirrels, fiendish foxes and raucous ravens, we are on to you!